Timeless

James Silva

Book and Cover design by James Silva

ISBN: 978-0-578-94062-5

First Edition: July 2021

10 9 8 7 6 5 4 3 2 1

Table of Contents

Foreword

This is one of my life's greatest honors, that this book would be held in your hands. I'm thankful for everything that had to happen in order to write this book, and I'm thankful that you have a copy. I hope you enjoy reading this story as much as I enjoyed writing it. I wish you the best in life, and I hope you find your way.

There are many beautiful things in this life, but there is nothing comparable to love. The more profound, the more difficult to see leave. The happiness in those sacred recollections is mirrored in the suffering that follows the loss of a truly special person, and many times, our perception of life can become a darkened echo of what it once was.

Life is a cycle, and all times, whether good or unpleasant, will pass. We shouldn't negate the latter, but rather accept them, learn, and be grateful for the sweetness within the hurt, because you will be able to go to your grave without the regret of not knowing what it truly means to love.

Introduction

The charm of a woman in a man's mind

Is inevitable from time to time

The heart will be broken,

Whether by love,

Or by word's left unspoken

Timeless

Chapter 1

It's not ideal, working in this factory,

sorting merchandise all day, a slave, practically

There are a lot of cool people here though,

who work and speak tactically,

but there are those who have faded here

over the past 20 years,

and continue to trade their lives for money, unhappily

I'm only here for a little while,

to make some cash and burn a few calories

The real passion lies in music and composing, actually

One of my frustrations has been the incremental rewards

that go to those who can barely fulfill their responsibilities

accurately

I'm working, giving the best of my strength, only to

see my wages thin drastically

None of the managers or supervisors can explain why

How would they know of such a thing?

I hate this, but I need the money

They laugh in secret, enlarging their pot of honey

I've come close to using profanity

These four walls are hunting for my sanity,

but it's just for now

I'll make it out of here somehow

At least at home I can get away from this for a while

It's not too far, only 36 miles

The second half of the school year is starting soon

I cherish my sleep, so I'll pick a class that starts at noon

Just one

Just for fun

I've been wanting to learn something new for a while

You can never have too many books,

and what a blessing it is when they start to pile

I would go on to learn many things,

and in this novel experience be drenched

Who would have known that

it was all going to happen while

studying the language of the French...

Day one

1:15PM

What a great way to start

I'm not irresponsible

I was ran over by a shopping cart,

or pulled over for having my windows tinted too dark.

Whichever works best.

I open the door, and the lecture goes on.

40 heads turn to look at the biggest moron.

The professor, thank God, was extremely kind.

I apologized afterwards, to which she responded

"Never mind. There's one seat available

in the back by the door. You can have it if

you promise not to be late anymore."

It's Wednesday, and so it begins

Pencil and paper, I withdraw from the leather skins

It's quiet, as it should be

The charcoal dances while the teacher speaks,

that is, until we get to the interactive part of the textbook.

The teacher asks for volunteers to re- enact the dialogue in

front of the class, so I try not to make eye contact or look.

I feign that I'm hyper- focused on my notes,

as if that would prevent the progress of this anecdote

"Miss, why don't you come to the board?"

The girl sitting a few rows in front of me rises and goes.

I push my tongue against the roof of my mouth,

slowly breathing,

as the desk indents the skin below my elbows.

It must be my lucky day.

But I just had to look up.

"Late boy, in the back."

Everyone laughs.

I went and stood in front of my new dialogue

partner and was softened as I looked

up from my lines.

Everything that is beautiful, the treasure of this age,

lay in her, confined.

Stunning, gorgeous, that would have been an insult.

11

Delicate, lovely, alluring…there is no proper definition for something this sublime

I rest and read under my tree after class

She walks by as I lay in the reed meadow grass

Solitude has been excellent company for several years' past

But perhaps love is being aroused, awakened at last

As the semester progressed,

I'd wonder if she ever noticed me, besides that day

It's not always easy to tell

We'd go our separate ways at the sound of the bell

In my experience, there are a few guidelines

to reference and consider in order to find out

if a woman is interested

Step 1: She's not

Many times I had mistakenly thought that

when someone has been overly kind,

affectionate, suggestive, and wanted to

get together to spend time,

they had a romantic interest in mind

I reckon that's not always the case

You're better off not knowing the taste of mace

But each time I saw her, she was all the more attractive,

and after a while, my defense mechanisms became inactive

Sapphire and emerald struggled in vain to separate themselves

from each other, and the result was the hue of her iris

Uncommonly intelligent, humble and pure

A siren, of unadulterated loveliness

An accurate description could not fit onto any amount of

papyrus

I pondered the different outcomes a lot,

and figured, regardless of the end result, it was worth a shot

I had to talk to her...

So I patiently waited for class to end

I waited for everyone to leave so I could catch up to her.

How I'd start the conversation, I wasn't sure.

I tapped on her shoulder and

as soon as I opened my mouth, I heard the teacher call-

She wanted to make sure I didn't forget my books,

and not only that, I was so fortunate that she also asked me

how I felt with the subject material overall

Next time I'll just dismiss myself early for "work"…

Being an adult comes with its perks

Thursday came and I skipped class.

I studied that day's chapter and waited in the library until

it was 2 o'clock. I nervously headed downstairs

towards the building closest to the soccer field.

My palms were already sweating, and

I wasn't sure I had enough courage,

but it was one of those things that you force yourself to do,

because you wouldn't be able to

live with yourself if you didn't see it through.

I walked over to the building and began having doubts

Everyone left, and when the professor locked her door

it was clear:

She wasn't even here.

Friday came and I decided to leave everything as is.

I was on my way to class, and there she was,

going in the opposite direction.

"Hey!"

She stopped and looked in my direction.

"Aren't you in my French class?"

- "Yes! And you sit in the back."

"Yeah, that's right. You're not going to class today?"

- "No, I have to go home to check on my grandmother."

" Is she alright?"

- "Yeah, she just needs me to pick up her medication, you know, and to see if she's fallen and can't get up."

"Wow…" I couldn't help but laugh. We continued on our conversation for several more minutes before I forced myself to tell her.

"Hey, I know you have to leave right now, but I would really like to see you again, outside of class."

- "Really? Well, you'll need my number then."

What…just…happened…

I had just done the impossible. I now had those immaculate digits.

All throughout the weekend I'd pull up her contact…

and start to fidget…

Phone calls…

I've never felt completely comfortable making them

It's probably where my lack of experience becomes

most evident,

where I sound like a fool, outside of my element

I'd rather ride a roller coaster,

or even jump in the tub with my favorite toaster

I'll see her in class on Monday anyways

I'll talk to her soon, in a few days

Class ended Monday and I went to find her.

"Hey!"

- "Oh, hey."

"How are you?"

- "Good."

"Those indefinite articles are really giving me a hard time. And those conjugations…What's wrong?"

- "Nothing… I just thought you'd call."

"I'm gay."

- "What?... Really?"

"Yeth."

Her laughter was my great reassurance.

"No, not really but now that I have your attention, I had something I wanted to ask you but I wanted to ask in person."

- "And what's that?"

"Would you like to get something to eat this weekend?"

- "Just like that?" That look on her face...

"Just like that. A scrumptious meal, and maybe a walk afterwards?"

- "...Sounds kind of nice. "

"Oh, it will be. When are you free?"

- "Depends."

"On?"

- "Whether or not you'll actually show up."

"I wouldn't do that to you... I wouldn't do that to anyone."

- "...because I was really disappointed this past weekend. I was really looking forward to talking to you."

"I'm sorry. To be honest I was a little nervous and don't like the sound of my voice over the phone. I prefer live interaction. I feel there's a lot of body language that is lost within the context of a phone conversation and those nuances help me to better understand the other person."

- "You actually have a very good point, so I'm not mad at you anymore. "

33

"Good, you better not be."

"Excuse me?

"You heard me."

Her laugh…her laugh…

I was so glad she knew how to take a joke.

"So, when are you free?

- "Yes. I mean, this Friday at 9!"

"Like AM or PM?"

- "If it's past your bedtime I completely understand."

"Hey I'm just making sure...I'll come for you Friday at 9. Well, I have to get to class, but I'll see you soon."

I offered her my curved right arm for a hug, and she offered me both of hers. It was the best feeling ever.

"Take care. I'll talk to you soon."

-"Sounds good. Call me."

3 days gone by

I'm getting nervous

I won't lie

Friday evening

6:30PM – Lunch break

30 minutes long

It's barely enough time for a pizza to bake

I'll just drive to a nearby burger stand

What?

Where's my car?

I know I didn't park it very far...

I guess dinner will be my lunch tonight

I wasn't even that hungry, just wanted something light

I'm on my way, I'm clocking out

As I exit, on the big screen lies a man who was once

champion, officially knocked out

I look in the parking lot until I remember it was stolen

8 hours on my feet

It's no wonder they're swollen

It's no biggie I guess

One of my co-workers

lives in the same direction anyways

I shower, dry off and change my clothes,

and take in my hand the most perfect rose

I leave the house, timing it just right,

and head to the bus stop across the street,

but the neighbor's dog thinks differently

It's been a while since anyone's given him his feed

My steps echo and the sound bounces

off of the adjacent houses

Please dog, not right now, don't make me fight

I can't be late, bow wow wow, I have a date tonight

Chapter 2

I knocked on her door with

a dry pulse in my neck

I had seen beauty before, but not like

that of her Greek semblance

We began our walk, and talked the whole way,

15 minutes of witty banter before thinking to ask

about her day

We placed our orders and paid no attention to the wait

Our silence was disrupted by laughter, her eyes shyly smiling

as I'd contemplate

Just by looking at me, you would have no idea how hungry

I was by that time

Each bite was as an answered prayer

Had I been alone, I would have eaten the way

kids eat a bag of gummy bears

We headed back to her home, unaware of the hour

The entire night had been consumed by a

dialogue of music, life, and

not a single second gone stale or sour

As we passed the town's clock tower, we were

welcomed by the cool air,

a clear sky, and a light meteor shower

We sat beside each other and continued to

 extract the reason from within our minds,

amusing ourselves with what we'd find

The longer we talked, the more it grew, this thought…

The thirst to know the curvature of your mouth

with that of my own, even if just once

Let me find rest in your heaven,

as the adrenaline makes several rounds throughout

The starlight drops below,

everything becomes slow, and

at last I know, that you've been thinking the same thing,

as we enjoy the after glow

Rarely have I ever lived what I would call a perfect night,

but this was absolutely one of them,

skipping all the way home under the lampposts and

street lights

There is a beauty that the eye has not yet beheld,

and upon seeing it, converts all else into a jail cell

I'm struck with awe,

and the tremendous fortune of having met her

the semester after fall

I awoke the next day ecstatic, but also worried

What if when I saw her again,

her recollection was blurry?

I hope she doesn't see me as a mistake

I'd just forget it ever happened, for both our sakes

The weekend comes to a close

The closer I get to our classroom, the more

the anticipation grows

I left as soon as we were dismissed,

And I heard her call my name

I turned to look, and behold

Her smile had not changed

We're going to the movies to see what's showing,

suppressing my excitement without you knowing

Making fun of the ones that are poorly made,

between the crunch of warm popcorn and sips of

raspberry Iced Tea lemonade

Her dark hair and fair skin,

More delicate than porcelain

The trips down to the countryside's creek,

with bread to feed the jittering beaks

To take her hand in mine at the park,

To spin her and pull her close after dark

Counting stars at night,

laying in the fields of wheat,

talking about anything,

in the summer heat

Sharing hot drinks and marshmallows with

the sudden downpour, and

getting lost together in the pages at the bookstore

I feel like I've known her forever

The value of this feeling is beyond measure

Each time I saw her was like the very first time

The elation, no matter how often, never died

Everything was an adventure

We enjoyed each other's company because we were both

determined to enjoy every second we'd have on this Earth

Every day was a new start, another rebirth

This weekend we'll be trying something different,

for a first-time's sake

We've accepted two tickets to the local

museum's annual art exhibit

A few of our mutual friends are going,

and this will be a great night,

as long as the moon keeps on glowing

It becomes increasingly difficult to concentrate on this
conversation,
when I notice the meaning in your eyes, and the
wetting of your lips, in that particular combination

Even from across the room you become my pure, insatiable,
innocent temptation,
and we laugh because no one can see the correlation
between our smiling and the bruises we each bear,
slightly noticeable but not lacerations

Staring at each other in silence, nothing is lost in translation
Being even a few inches away from your incessant allure is
the source of my vexation

But I'm satisfied, even to lightly penetrate your thoughts,
like paper seeping with ink blots

Chapter 3

I wonder what she's up to right now...

Reading perhaps, or sketching in a quiet room

At least we have that in common,

gravitating towards similar things, in which we find our

peace and calm in

Spinning, the vibrations orbit the needle

Edison's cunning, safe from the times of the Medieval

Outside, the dark green pasture leans forward with

the rush of cool air

Radiant bloom is imminent; it's going to rain

I can see it from my rocking chair

Deep colors drip from the gramophone

If it weren't for you in my thoughts, I'd be here alone

Out the window the scenery looks incredibly nice,

through the smoke of the coconut curry and

the steamed white rice

And one day I'd be honored if you tried it

Come over, once the wine runs out from our picnic basket

Stay long enough for us to become moonlit,

laughing, poking fun at each other,

conversing on your being a recent graduate,

and my being abstinent,

as you search for condiments in my lowest cabinets,

wearing a dress, with nothing underneath on,

knowing I might look all along…

I could never be bored with her

As long as we were together, we would have a great time,

of that I was sure

There's a beautiful valley, a hidden place that she knows of

and would like to show me

It's close to the beach and is laden with fruit trees

How could I say no?

Besides, there was a discount that week for

anyone taking the metro

Chapter 4

The sound of this beach could not be more perfect

I could see it over the green hills as we got off on our stop

The water was a deep blue turquoise, and would wash away

small rocks, shells and flip flops

The sand bore a light tan,

retaining most of its natural white

A joyous sound of friends and family having a great time,

while the birds called as they'd take flight

The surfers would pass by those playing volleyball,

and none of us had any other care in the world at all

Even after several hours I remain possessed by this

never-ending scene of nature

Surrounded by all this beauty, especially

standing next to me,

I think to myself that there must be a Creator

I'm pondering this when I vaguely hear her

mention a lovely cottage that only she knows of

It's set to be torn down

I noticed in her voice a small frown

I don't want to see her like that so we go,

and she shows me all of the trees along the way that bare

bananas, blueberries, and mangos

We would have to cross the river without

anything to dry ourselves with

There are a few homes on the hills,

fenced by ropes and clothes pins

The clear stream combs around the pebbles,

chiseling the stones

We waited, and waded until it was obvious that

we were alone

We carried on our conversation until the

quiet was enough

On occasions that turned into laughter and a

deep gaze, as I'd twist the water from my shirt,

unrolling the cuffs

We escaped off the walking trail and went to

where the birds flew,

and you invited me to feel along your dress,

still damp with water, which was now see- through

The tips of my fingers lightly trace your mandible,

and I use my lips to soften the tender of your neck

My passion and patience right now are incompatible,

like love, and any logic that can be rational

The wooden floor is replenished

from the dripping of my fingertips

The contours of your body I have found, without blemish

As the eagerness is sucked from your lips to mine,

the sound of footsteps blends with the song of the coastline

Someone might be coming, but our gazes agree

Making this any shorter would be the only travesty

If there ever was an expression of love,

in what other way could I express it more sincerely?

Each motion becomes increasingly vehement,

and we quiver against each other,

warmed by the sunlight bleeding through the

half-opened shutters

The room, now silent, is fragrant with

hibiscus and Molly's white,

as we wander and search the constellations

hidden in each other's eyes

Chapter 5

Week after week,

month after month,

I'm sinking deeper and deeper,

betting everything I have,

unafraid to challenge the cards dealer

There's no bliss like that of the first kiss,

nothing as sacred, as persuasive, as her nakedness,

and her thought follows me across distance, through time,

in this boundless empirical paradigm

My heart tests the strength of my rib cage

and I live in happiness,

glad to awaken every morning,

with a spirit no longer ravenous

Her laughter is as the ocean

As soon as I hear it, nothing can hide my smile

It's like the scent of cotton and fabric softener

in my clothes, folded in a pile

It's like the sound of music

bouncing off black and white tiles

It's medicine for us both, uncontainable in a vial

A sound so pure, in which there is no beguile

When reality is better than a dream,

you're so cautious, as not to tear the

present at any of the seams

Playful fondling at golden hour,

Pollenating among the flowers

That which allows me to speak, wanders,

from your ankles to the inner of your thighs

A sound so dulcet, that nature pries

I savor every indent along the curve of your spinal column

Adagio, lentando, religiously, and solemn

Forward and back, until I'm graced by the

blushing that shows me I'm correct,

enraptured and entranced,

in the company of Bill Evans' take on Brubeck

You've become short of breath,

and so draws nigh, la petite mort,

the most beautiful of deaths

Butter, cinnamon, dark cane sugar lips

Deeper in savor than lightly honeyed apple crisps

Biting, only until an incision becomes possible

Pleasure is love's opioid, revealing the

natural crimson in our cheeks,

as we look into each other,

aware and docible

The blood of blueberries from a frozen cluster

is my favorite drink, until your lips can no longer utter

Your hair rests within my reach,

lured by the vigor of its pull,

my hands grasping you, wherever my hands are full

Your voice is gentle and wordless,

at times being heard throughout the plains,

becoming the guest in my mind

when I sit by the colors of glass stained,

so frequently, that a reminder isn't required,

and there is no need of energy,

while love has not yet expired

The blanket of warmth scours my back

Time has left us to be alone, and we've lost track

This feeling swells as the body tastes of heaven,

in the culmination of our youth and essence

Having not met you any sooner will forever be my

greatest transgression

I've spilled my ink onto your canvas

and we've become each other's quill

Go ahead, my love, write whatever you will

Drink of my cup until you've had your fill,

of all this water, pure and distilled

Leave me not, as one who plucks the daffodils

Leave me not, lest by your absence I become ill

James Silva

All throughout the day you occupy my mental frame,

and removing you from it would leave me as

one who has been maimed

The bright sky awakens me in the mornings,

and I'm happier than anyone could ever be,

with new radiance as I carry you inside me

Oh, how my colors resound,

when I wear you as my crown

To your voluptuousness, and yours only, do I

find myself bound

95

The candles burn, and

the wax embalms my hands

The soul yearns beyond the funnel of the sand

The most beautiful,

the most delicate

You make hard the will to be celibate

Stay a little longer

You are the good in my life

You are the warmth in my bed

You run through me as the color red

The dopamine has faded

Disregard the early hour,

for my pupils thirst to be dilated,

covering your mouth so that we won't be much louder,

as our bodies become condensated

Perspiring over your temple,

as I rediscover the threshold of the afterlife

and convulse within you, intertwined,

as our breathing becomes abbreviated,

and next to you I lay, sedated

The sound comes from outside the window pane

Dark skies that can no longer retain

the prayers of the ground,

water undetained

Each drop hits the roof and overlays us with

the mellow downpour

Our only option for warmth is our proximity,

using only one candle to see, because

there is no electricity

How can I, myself contain,

when the night ending too soon is your only complaint

This euphoria, you've freely given me,

and I return it to you, inflicting your favorite pain,

offering you my passion, unrestrained,

as hours fade, in the seduction of the rain

Summer walks by the lake

Fall grass combed by the rake

Opening my eyes to the bottom half of my window

caked by snowflakes

Spring's banana- chocolate crepes

Holding you as you asked,

against the wall, covered in drapes

Finding stability, making myself tall,

absorbing every minute detail, as one does with

the satisfaction in the brittle of a grape

You are what makes any of this matter,

expending all of our strength, to the point

where we can only stagger, and

suffocate in laughter

I thought I'd never feel this way again,

that I'd be so happy when I'd tell you I want to see you and

you'd happily ask "When?"

At the very thought of you my knees become feeble

I see you whenever I see the town steeple

I have something I hope she'll like

I'm careful not to drop it while riding my bike

It's something that goes around her neck,

and fits in her pocket

It's the prettiest one I could find,

a one-of-a kind locket

Looking onwards, content to be seeing you

later on in the day,

Gallantly striding down the steps, hearing in my head

the partitas and the bourrée

Eager for your eyes to rest on each of the

petals in this bouquet,

and offer you a serenade, by the waters where

the swans play

I've just bought bread and wine, clearly too excited that I'd

almost forgotten to pay

These moments reach deeper into the confines of my mind

every time I let them replay

Oh…no… that's ok

This hardly ever happens anyway

I don't want to tell her how I feel,

just for her to see me dismayed

It's a small price to pay to conserve our peace

In the end I had only driven halfway

Strange, she never works on Thursdays

Chapter 6

Seven days have gone by,

and the anticipation is even greater

I write to her to ask if…

And she'll get back to me later…

14 days have expired,

and I know I won't be disappointed again,

but she completely forgot, and

tonight, she'll be with her friends

I strain my eyes to see what's wrong

You're too kind, so you play along,

until we're around other people,

and I know exactly where I don't belong

An honest answer

is all I want

An honest answer

in any kind of font

This time it's on my end

My boss is short -staffed, and he won't bend

I have to stay and work an extra shift

Three hundred more boxes to lift,

Three hundred more boxes to sift

To find the chance to see each other is

becoming like hide and seek

I know it's because we both have

our responsibilities but it's been five weeks...

Tired of all this, I let the ringing in my ear take over

Drained, I can't feel anything,

not even your cold shoulder

I need to quit this job soon

There's no reward, except struggling

against the fate of a loon

I just don't understand,

how your responses can be so bland

Your undying effort to ignore me is truly flattering

This whole act of being ok, I'm really mastering

There's not enough common sense that I can gather

What's wrong with wanting to hear from you

a few days faster?

Of course, there are always multiple factors,

but if you do care, why are you such a talented actor?

This has become a dark chapter

I'm waiting for you like an unemptied bladder

Your skin has dissolved into mine

The discomfort of your pulling away

is the indication, the sign

I feel it when you're not around

You're pushing me deeper into the ground

Chapter 7

Finally! An answer!

I read what you've sent me,

no need for my optic enhancer

It's such a long message,

and I can't believe it's actually here

I remember it well, as the greatest

turning point of that year

I'm almost at the end, and the lines are running out

There has to be some hesitation, some angst,

some goodwill in here, even if only a small amount

But it is all mine... while you sound like

you're doing just fine

None of this makes any sense

You have me worded in the past tense

I wouldn't say I love you

Unless I was sure

I wouldn't say I love you

As a temporary cure

I wouldn't say I love you

Unless I was sure,

that I could spend 70 years beside you without

missing who you were

What can I say?

Is this an illusion?

I wish it were so, but you've already

reached your conclusion

What you want and what's best

don't usually coincide, you say,

but the worst part is where you

tell me your feelings haven't changed,

and that to think that you don't love me

anymore would be absurd

I guess I'll believe whatever speaks louder

between your actions and your words

I'm...really happy for whoever ends up by your side

This is an unusual surprise, completely out of the blue

I don't know what to say, or what happens next,

but... you can be sure that I'll be missing you

I guess that's it…

I should just allow myself to be

swallowed by the bottomless pit…

No...not like this...

All that time, all those experiences,

all of the happiness, all of the fun,

every touch, every secret...

We're just going to act like they never happened?

It can't end like this...

What if all she's looking for is to see if I'll

try to change her mind...

But I could never...

Once someone has chosen to leave,

I've decided to let them...

Either someone wants you or they don't...

But...

What if this is the only thing keeping me from

a lifetime spent with my beloved?

Is this self-respect or is this pride?

I can live with rejection, but not regret...

How should I go about this?

Chapter 8

A box of chocolates

How could that fail?

Well, apparently it can…

At least I'll have a nice snack to enjoy…

I don't get it

You would think this gesture would endear,

rather than annoy…

No, this time I have it! I have the real solution!
New hope invigorates me as I leave the
warehouse of central distribution
I repeat it loudly between my ears,
over and over in my mind
But the F repels the arrow to the E,
And my debit card is declined

It's a good thing I have a wrinkled Abe,
washed and dried in my pocket,
with some leftover change I had forgotten
I removed from my wallet

I pass the 3rd city and I'm already very near
The delight in your voice will be so precious to hear
I park on the hill and begin my descent
Your house is on the very bottom
Please don't despise this humble attempt

She will, I know it, she will come to her window

and invite me out of this dark limbo

I hope within myself, for love, and for resolution

Cradled in my arms is the sound of the Baroque, and

dark jazz, played by my guitar, who's

wood is Andalusian

My fingers pluck perfectly, a piece of my own

People walk out on their balconies in

robes that are foreignly sewn

Some, to experience the music, and some to be alone

Others, with three numbers already dialed on their phone

The final note resonates,

and it's not what I expected

My lips are parched, and

it's becoming a familiar feeling, this feeling of being dejected

I rest the guitar in its case and leave when I'm done

No response at all for this audience of one

There remains one more candle in my heart, still inscended

This was all a mistake, but I had not yet repented

You are completely different than when I first met you

My thoughts that were already lopsided,

are now divided in two

I'm amazed at what my eyes are seeing,

forcing a smile with internal bleeding

It's difficult to understand you from this range

You leave me to close the distance

with borrowed change

This will be the 3rd time I've knocked on your door

An hour's journey, and a little more

Well - received by silence, I should have better known,

to have packed an extra set of sneakers to get back home

Now the sky has darkened, and I've gone

almost half the way

The mist of the night will eventually leak

the dawn of the day

With hills on both sides, the Domenigoni

appears and hides

Further down the road, the valley fits

perfectly into the sky

The orange groves, citrus leaves and bushes

extend for miles

Ramona lays quietly sleeping, her swings swaying,

reminding me of the piles of woodchips, monkey bars,

and lining up outside in a single file

Acacia has always taken me this far,

but there's this other street that glistens and gleams,

flickering romantically when the cobblestone and rain meet

Harvard remains as it always has, antiquated

I've walked it many times in good spirits, and

many times frustrated

Continuing on to my left is that park, preserving some

good times from when I was very young

There's a name carved by my brother in the tower,

20 years past and touched by no one

I've reached the end of the city and

I put my key in the door

It fits perfectly but won't slide anymore

Disillusioned, I observe the city for one last time

The haven is gone, and so am I

I cry, because it's not the same

Without any notice, everything has already changed

So it looks like I'll be moving

I'm tired of lacking, tired of losing,

tired of a life that others are choosing

Chapter 9

So there it is…

That is it

I'm one more blurry face on the public transit,

having trouble removing my eyes from the floor,

while accepting that you have no love for me anymore

The void has become vacant

and I feel nothing

I'm glad to see you, but

you observe me as undistinguished,

uninteresting, and disgusting

Now let the blood keep dripping,

and take your time as you keep sipping

on my life, but gently, as I feel it slipping

Your smile has become crippling,

so hurry and spit me out like a fingernail clipping

It hurts to breathe, and I inhale begrudgingly

How can I call this life? I'm alive but barely

I exist silently

My eyes are the marquee

There are no tickets left anymore, I'm so different

I can't even see me

I'm tired, depleted

I just want to go home,

to listen to music,

to see a message on my phone

5 days in a row, and now finally comes the weekend

I'll be able to see my family,

and maybe a few friends

Far from being rich,

but I finally have a spare dollar to spend

My coworkers and I have just been liberated

by the opening gate

It's almost midnight because we all stayed late

Good luck leaving the parking lot anytime soon

No one knows how to wait in line…

Baboons

There goes another 10 minutes, just waiting my turn

Some people never learn

Eventually, we pour out onto the empty streets

I'm going straight home

I'm too tired to look for something to eat

I'm willing to ignore my stomach's growling

in exchange for a few more moments of sleep

I debate whether or not I'll shower

Was the water shut off, or do I still have another hour?

I drive the way I always do,

windows down, observing the city view

I swear I did nothing wrong when my steering wheel

turned shades of red and blue

That's what I hate about quotas,

and someone who thinks I don't know

who I'm talking to

My innocence has been rewarded, and now

I have a citation that's in 3 months due

I covet the iris upon which your

countenance is being engraved,

and envy him who to you has found himself enslaved,

because it's the sweetest thing until it ends

It's the sweetest thing when you pretend

Lips

Irreplaceable, unobtainable

Inviting, Inciting, Inclining

How deceptive, ambiguous, misleading, and false-hearted is

Cupid's bow

Return to me, my love, return to me

Bring me back an olive branch, pure dove

Return to me

Sorrow continues to roll down the calendar,

taking me farther away from your bed of lisianthus, and

Rosa Midnight, your lovely parameter

If only I were a time- traveler

I'd go back to when your only attire was

the aroma of lavender

I'm eager to see you, and tired of being a janitor

Correspondence…still empty, but I'll wait

Over on the balcony, where I can see over the gate

Maybe it's just a few hours late

Eventually, you'll come back and we'll share a dinner plate

Books, I've gone through an entire stack

Actually, I'm surprised you haven't asked for them back

Collections of incredible art and stories

Krispy Kreme receipts hidden like an allegory

More often that I thought, I've become the fool

You're grasping the reins, and I'm the mule

Longing, and longing, it's

Obvious I feel out of my natural habitat

Victory alludes me, and it's sad

Even a good man at times, is mistaken for a door mat

If I were to admit that I still miss you…

You would laugh, and see me as pathetic

A reprobate, emotional anorexic

I can't…just to be made a mockery, and endure slander,

to make my greatest effort again, just to become a

parable for the bystanders…

If you could endure what I've felt,

You would perceive me with new eyes

Your blankets would be cold as you stack them at night

The moon would turn away, and make known

its indifference, and hide the stars

You would become a charlatan,

trying only to enjoy your favorite candy bar,

and seeing me smile would bring out the scars,

because I would seem deceptively happy, keeping you afar

Another day, another breath

Another chance to see what's left

So then, I lay down to sleep,

for perhaps by the shutting of my eyes can our souls meet

At times, I awake suddenly because my stomach falls,

thinking I have seen a faceless moving rag doll,

but when fortunate, I return to your fountain

and swim as far as I can, however deep

The possibility of a successful dive is as common as

a year that leaps

The dreamland is barren and crunches with dry leaves

I awaken tired every morning, for

the laboring farmer has many a time sown,

without the guarantee that he'll ever reap

I seek rest, but haven't found it

My dreams torment me

My darkened eyes will be the first to admit

I hear children, amused at something,

gathering quickly, rushing

There I see you standing in the opposite line

I guess we're next, in this big backyard in the

apartment complex

I thought I had played this game before, but

I should have asked, and now I can't

back out anymore

Blind-folded, we spin and calculate,

aiming for the center, aiming to amputate

Circled by a restless crowd,

a last breath will be drawn tonight by 8

Sweat congregates in my handkerchief

My shirt is nowhere to be found

I keep swinging until my knife meets the sound

of a crunch or a tear

Only then can I fully penetrate, and leave it

stuck in the ground

But something doesn't feel right

Your breathing is stable

Now who is Cain, and who is Abel?

Your steps follow mine

No deviations, only a straight line

The sand is ungrateful, not yet satisfied,

because despite the flow of blood, no one has yet died

All around, the laughter augments

The time has come

It's the end of Lent

I lay down for my last time and

uncover my eyes in this earthen bed

Not a scratch on you, not even a band around your forehead

Again I close my eyes and open them once lucid

What I see is terrible and makes me all the more reclusive

I'm forced to watch, and feel, within this nightmare

I must have thought about you too much…

I'm not sure how much more I can bare

I don't want to look, because I know what's coming next…

You're about to leave with him…

I want to know who you're with but you deflect

Foreign satisfaction has come, for your purity to collect

Let the reel run out so there's no more pain to project

It almost does me no good to continue caring for you,

as you keep throwing my emotions in your pot of stew

Why do I fall for it?

Under the sun, nothing is ever new

Everyone seems to have life working out for them,

while I feel like I missed out, and have been left behind,

as if I'm frozen, inanimate within a moment,

as if it were the last day of school and I was the last to leave

No proper goodbye's, sleeping in my car on New Year's Eve

Droplets of rain tap and blur the windows as I think

of all the bitterness I've had to drink,

but I offer myself encouragement;

Eventually, someday, it will be alright

Try and sleep well tonight, for tomorrow is Valentine's

Your smile, I fear that it has found refuge in

someone else…

The heat is gone from your arms,

but what have I done?

I've loved too much

There must be a solution, some sort of remedy

for the pain

I've become the town fool, trying to walk

with both my ankles sprained

It's either I fade into the music or into you

Between life and death, it's difficult to see any

difference between the two

Chapter 10

Memories are my only keepsake

A portal to the past, a trip that only I can take,

but I can't stay there,

with my hands running through your hair,

because I wouldn't want to come back,

from the place in life where I felt I had everything, to the

current place where you are everything,

and everything is what I lack

It's all too easy to misunderstand,

so I'm angry when you offer me a helping hand

I've tried to reduce your image in me,

and learn to live carelessly,

but I can not

It's not as easy as I thought

The soul is a scholar, and yearns,

for the more you ignore him, the more he learns

I have to move on, and scrape off this anguish;

Rediscover life so it won't remain tasteless

To know what it's like for your soul to long for another,

for the five senses to be amplified,

is to discover a gold mine…

A person is fortunate to experience this even once

in their lifetime

And I cry gratefully,

for having experienced it for myself…

I remember you on days where I go about casually

To suppress these memories would be blasphemy,

but I always consider beforehand, because

wanting to go back and re-live them has been

my everlasting incapacity

In tasting you, I have tasted spirituality

I fear not death, but the lack of you that

would be made apparent by immortality

At times I wonder if I'm missed,

if you've preserved the taste of our last kiss,

or if you've forgotten

the uncommon spring blossom,

as you drown me in this abyss

Does love ever really die?

Maybe it runs off for a little while and hides

in the fantasies of would-be brides

It wanders off until you're healed and don't need to lie

It watches from a distance as a passerby,

and will avoid you until you're finished asking why

Life goes on

With only good in my heart for you...so long...

I want you to have an amazing life

I'm ready to lay to rest this internal strife

Chapter 11

It's been several years since that day

These thoughts are surfacing with the setting sun and

the ocean spray

I served my time, and I'm not posting any more bail

I've left all my troubles and secretly set sail

You hoped to never see me again, so I've disappeared

I can only hope that you'll change your mind

in a few years

What will you be like when this letter reaches you?

Will you remember me? Would you even read it,

at least a poem or two?

When I think of you, how could I be irate, or at all upset?

My fingers still caress you,

hidden underneath the strings,

in each one of my guitar's frets

The thought of you seeps through the pen,

and is raveled in my melodies,

together once again, staring at each other breathlessly

I want to savor summer on my skin, and

run into you at the pier to ask you how you've been,

Tantalize each other in reminiscence,

ponder how the years have not

touched any of your brilliance,

and how you can meet me again after so long,

and make glad the memory of my existence

Forgive me, for in my pursuit I became masochistic

I had not yet inherited the wisdom to understand,

but I owed it to myself to be persistent

Had I not done that, I would have

lived on with the regret…

"What if I had tried to win her back?"

So romantic on paper, so foolish in the act

And as soon as you come,

I know it'll already be time to go

The universe is conducting us at different tempos

The night is pushing us toward each other,

starry, just as it was with Van Gogh,

but Andante is not Adagio

I believe we'll catch up to each other in the end,

but in the meantime, these are all the words I wrote,

but could never send

I would have, but fate prohibited me from doing so…

I will always be grateful for all of the shared happiness…

Every part of you, I will always save,

and they will always be safely buried,

for I am your grave

If you ever happen to hear my guitar,

or see something familiar in this memoir…

How interesting

The theory of the red string

Perhaps, you are not too far

If I ever found your fingerprints on my cookie jar,

or a glimmer of hope in your reservoir,

bitter would be sweet,

when our souls again meet…

Look at all that has become of your au revoir

…Finally …

The sun has resurrected and shimmers again

I knew that one day lovesickness would

finally be drained from the pen

I can see color after so long,

and hear the music in life that had been long gone

All is not lost

At last I can smile

The heart will never again sink if you were to

visit the docks, or if your image should visit

me in my thoughts

I sit on the bench by the lakeside,

where most hours of the days I spend,

deciphering the great works of Buxtehude, Bach,

Beethoven, and Robert Cummings, all friends

184

After a long day of studying, relying on

the shade as my clock,

The willows fawn over the gates of the

houses on each block

I pass them by on my way home

Briskly I go, and every now and then because

what a nice surprise it would be,

If while I prepared supper, you were

waiting outside when the door knocks,

happy to see me...

Socks freshly washed and dried

warm me on my couch with some apple pie

I sit down and think as I press the pencil,

at times hard, at times gentle

This story is coming to an end, that is all

I'm ready to jump

I'm ready to fall

I'm almost late…

I'll be doing a concert tonight

I have to finish getting ready

The unforgettable moment,

the apple cider and a stage full of confetti are all waiting…

But...

When I remember you, I will look upon you with good eyes, and remember your smile, and your kindness, despite the disagreements...

The sacred part of your soul that you shared with me, and the beauty of who you are, will outlast the span of our lifetimes, and your handwriting in me will forever be timeless...

I hope someday you find this

The strands of the wheat fields call out to me,

to come and remember what it's like to be free

The sun, beating around her lace,

invoking the desire for one last taste

I'm not worried at all in the least

There's no danger whatsoever,

except that by seeing you after so long,

I would fall in love with a stranger forever

About The Author

Hi! My name is James Silva. I'm a composer, producer, arranger, musician, and author who is passionate about creating with substance, quality and excellence.

If you enjoyed this book, feel free to leave me a review!

And, if you enjoyed this poetry, you can find even more of it in my music, which is available across all streaming platforms, such as Spotify, Apple Music, Itunes, and YouTube.

One more thing! If you'd like your book signed, feel free to reach out at one of my shows and I'd be more than happy to sign it!

IG: @jamessilvamusic

Facebook: James Silva Music

Translations of selected songs

Paraíso

Her shirt became unbuttoned,

And our patience dwindled

To drink of you is to drink of the most delicious

To drink of you is to drink longing

Your words will be shortened as I slowly undress you,

You are the most sacred literature,

Music reincarnated

And when our time has come to an end,

How will I be able to remove you from myself?

Would it be possible?

I'm getting lost in the paradise of your temple,

Losing myself in your secret labyrinth,

Falling into a wishing well,

Losing myself in the perfection of this moment

I want everything with you,

But as time passes by, I don't see how that can be

This bothers you, but only a little

And now being with you is being alone

Verão

Summer, the time of love

How the heart beats

When the sun envelopes you

Your beauty, a gift from God

Linen and wine

The sand and the sea

It could not be any better

What a shame that everything has an end,

That all things must come to an end

Summer, the time of love

How the heart beats

When we find ourselves alone

Without any inhibition

Linen and wine

The sand and the sea

It could not be any better

What a shame that everything has an end,

That all things must come to an end

Summer, the time of love

How the heart beats

Every time that I remember that August

How we trembled,

Making ourselves belong to each other

It could not have been any better

What a shame that everything has an end,

That all things must come to an end

Brasileira

Mahogany and nylon call unto the waters of Brazil,
And I know that they only visit the island to see you,
Quetzal Xochitl

I want to see you, I want to feel you
I want to always know that all this is for me
The jasmine on your neck knows how to persuade me
Sabrosa muñequita
I want to see you, I want to feel you
I want to always know that all this is for me
How beautiful the craving in your moan, and
What rich poetry

There is a proverb that keeps eluding me
And I don't understand it because you keep consuming me

I want to see you, I want to feel you

I want to always know that all this is for me

You are the rose of which the hummingbird sings

The nectar of a guava

I want to see you, I want to feel you

I want to always know that all this is for me

Until I drink/take you I won't be able to sleep

And I want every last drop

If only you knew how you tempt me

That the evening becomes more vibrant as I know the

Bliss of being your lover

Incomparable

The fragrance of the orange groves remains engraved in me
and the sound of this fountain where I met you,

Bound to eternity
Baptized in serenity

Your eyes are able to leave me without words
and I know no greater pleasure
than when we are alone and I begin reading the prose
of your figure

And a sunset doesn't compare
Nor does the sweetness of honey

Or the flower when it blooms

Nothing compares to the taste of your skin

The air of the cathedral brought me here,

where the instrumental ensemble painted you

Lastímame

I'll take you to our heaven
Where there is no time, and on your lips I die

But gradually our souls separate, and
How it hurts to exist
Gradually our souls become untied
Why are you destroying me again?

Look at me bleed out
I can't reach you
How is it that you're leaving?
Stay and hurt me a little more

Sweet and asphyxiating is our suffering
Every time more penetrating

Every time more intense

But gradually our souls separate, and

How it hurts to exist

You thank me for understanding you

You're welcome

Why are you destroying me again?

Chica de Los Lentes

You've been very pensive

as the flour rises,

and these streets of old stones

have serenated us with their melancholy

But now it's time to close

and no one can see us here

I've been wanting to ask you about something that

fascinates me

If the light were turned off, would you take them off?

I would like to know

What is there behind your glasses,

your innocent semblance?

The moonlight is enough, and the desire is obvious

I want to lose my breath upon your mouth

and spill my passion over you,

navigate your oceans if life will return you to me

I think about it night and day

I want to intoxicate you with my caresses

But I'm on an extended wait

Until I feel your porcelain hands

But now it's time to close

and no one can see us here

I've been wanting to ask you about something that

fascinates me

If the light were turned off, would you resist me?

I would like to know, my love